The Super Skateplank

Peter Corey

Illustrated by Paul Longcrove

Chapter 1 - Ben's dream

Oooooh yeess!!! Up the ramp, down the ramp, each time going faster. Some twists, some turns, then a *Fakie Ollie* and a *Dormer Stormer* finish!

The crowd went wild – all six of them. Well, not wild exactly. Cassie shouted, "Well done, Ben!" (Cassie's my friend, but NOT a *girl friend*.) Brad shouted, "That's still a rubbish skateboard!" (Brad is not a friend of *any* sort.) OK, maybe it's not the coolest board on the planet. My dad made it out of some old roller skates and a plank. I call it my 'Super Skateplank'. Even Brad has to admit that it really rocks when it comes to doing stunts.

I'm Ben Dormer and I'm nine. A *Fakie Ollie* is a backwards jump, in case you didn't know. And a *Dormer Stormer* is my own special back flip.

I want to tell you about the skateboarding competition. There was a crowd of us at the skate park. We started talking about the competition that was happening the following week. Somebody said that we had to sign up at the sports centre.

"Let's do it!" I said.

Do you believe in love at first sight? I'm not talking soppy stuff. I'm talking about seeing the skateboard of your dreams. It was on display in the sports centre – first prize for the winner of the competition!

FIRST PRIZE!

SUPER-COOL
SKATEBOARD
STATE-OF-THE-ART
TOP-OF-THE-RANGE

Brad told the man behind the desk that he might as well give it to him right now because he was sure to win.

"He's not as good as Ben!" Cassie said.

"So, are you going to enter this competition, Ben?" the man asked kindly.

"Yes, please," I told him. He looked at me and smiled. Then he looked at my board and laughed.

"Not on that thing," he said. "Only proper skateboards are allowed – for health and safety reasons."

"What?" I was gutted.

"Don't worry," Cassie told me, "you can share mine."

"No, he can't," the man said firmly. "The rules are very clear: one person, one board, and no sharing."

"Never mind, Plankboy!" Brad sneered. "I *might* let you look at the board once I've won it!"

I could feel the sting of tears at the back of my eyes. That board was the coolest thing I'd ever seen and I had to win it. But without a proper board of my own I stood no chance.

Chapter 2 - Skater for hire

I needed to buy a proper board but nobody in our family had any money. The gardening was Dad's idea.

"I bet Mrs Thompson would let you tidy her garden," he said.

Mrs Thompson lived next door and her garden was like a jungle. She was delighted to have it tidied.

I worked *all day* Saturday. I found frogs, snails, half a bicycle and an ant's nest – but no tigers or lions. I also made no money.

"Did you tell her you wanted to be paid?" Dad asked. I had to admit that I'd forgotten that detail. So, after all my hard work, I was no closer to buying my own board. With the competition only a week away, I was getting desperate.

I spent Sunday running errands. Or rather, skating errands. Cassie helped me. All day we dashed back and forth to the corner shop to get people's newspapers and groceries and stuff.

When the shop shut, we sat on the wall outside and counted our earnings. Even though Cassie said I could keep her share, I still only had five pounds and thirty-two pence. Cassie worked out how long it would take us to make enough money to buy a skateboard.

"Six months," she told me. Cassie's pretty good at maths, so I had to believe her.

"It's hopeless!" I said and a heavy silence sat between us.

Suddenly Cassie said, "What about using Jake's board?"

Jake is my brother. He's fourteen, so you don't upset him if you want to live. But he did have a board. He'd thrown it into the back of the garden shed a few months ago, after falling off it. Maybe Jake would lend it to me. It was worth a try. It was also the only hope I had of being in the competition.

"No way!" Jake said when I asked him.

I tried to reason with him. "You don't even use it any more!"

Jake stormed off. Then, a few minutes later, came back with his board. He almost threw it at me. He hissed, "If anything happens to it, you are *history*." He meant it.

Later, Dad explained to me how much the board meant to Jake. He had worked hard and saved his money for a long time to buy it. He was a good skater – better than me – but when he fell off, it hurt his pride. (I'm sure that's not all he hurt!)

"What did you say to get Jake to lend it to me?" I asked.

"That's between Jake and me," said Dad, tapping his nose. "Just make sure you take really good care of it."

It was now less than a week before the competition. I practised every day after school. Cassie made up a training schedule. This is how it worked:

MONDAY: *Get used to Jake's board.*

This involved a lot of falling off!

TUESDAY: *As Monday.*

More falling off, followed by frantic checking of the board for damage. Jake's warning was still ringing in my ears.

WEDNESDAY: *Create routine.*

By now I could handle Jake's board pretty well. But without some flashy stunts, I still had no chance of winning. I decided to try my special *Dormer Stormer*. It's not easy on my skateplank but on Jake's board …

I pushed off from the top of the half-pipe, down the slope, up the other side, into the flip then – flat onto my bottom.

Brad was there to snigger.

"You better not break it, Plankboy," he warned. "If you do, Jake will flip higher than that board."

I did not need reminding. I did need more practice.

THURSDAY: *Dry run.*

This meant practising the moves until I could do them in my sleep. But it rained, so I went to bed and dreamed about them instead.

FRIDAY: *Final polish.*

This was meant to be a last chance to polish up my moves. Unfortunately everyone else had the same idea. I only got on the pipe for about two minutes.

"You've got no chance tomorrow!" Brad said with an evil grin.

SATURDAY: *Competition day!*

"You'll be fine," Dad told me.

"Try not to fall off," Mum added, ruffling my hair, which I hate!

Jake just glared and I got the message.

I grabbed my pads and helmet and headed for the skate park. I stopped off to buy a bottle of water on the way. That's when disaster struck!

Skateboards were not allowed in the shop, so I propped Jake's board up outside. After all, I would only be a few minutes. But by the time I got back outside, the board had gone!

What was I going to do? Without Jake's board, I couldn't be in the competition. That meant I had no chance of winning the state-of-the-art skateboard.

Still, none of this mattered, because without Jake's board, I was doomed!

Chapter 4 – Racing to win

There are two types of skaters. *Pipe* skaters use skate parks. *Street* skaters skate anywhere they like. I knew none of the pipe skaters would *dare* take Jake's board. So it must have been a streeter. I checked my watch. I had an hour to find Jake's board and get to the competition.

I sneaked home to pick up my skateplank (hoping not to bump into Jake). Then I headed for the building site by the canal. It was the perfect place for street skating. It had ramps, bits of wall, even metal bars to grind along. It was deserted. Everywhere else I looked was deserted too. All the skaters were already at the skate park.

I was running out of time. The only place I hadn't looked was the shopping centre.

I got there twenty minutes later. It was packed with shoppers, but there were no skaters. As I pushed through people on the escalator, a security man called to me, "Hey! No skating in here!"

There was no time to explain so I just said, "Sorry," and left. That was it. I'd run out of places to look.

Then I saw Cassie. "What are you doing here? Do you know what time it is?" she cried. I explained what had happened. Not only was I out of the competition but I was also doomed.

"You should still turn up at the skate park," Cassie told me. She was right. I ought to go there and explain why I couldn't take part.

As we arrived, they were calling my name. A grumpy judge stood on a platform at the top of the main half-pipe. He was tapping his clipboard impatiently. "Are you Ben Dromer?" he asked.

"*Dormer*, yes, but …"

"Well, get on with it," Grumpy told me. "We haven't got all day!"

"Go for it, Ben!" Cassie called out.

So I launched myself down the slope of the half-pipe. I expected one of the officials to shout, "That's not a proper skateboard!" but none of them did. So I went into my first *Fakie Ollie*, did a few turns, then into my *Dormer Stormer*. The crowd went wild – really wild – this time.

Then I saw it.

Leaning against a tree nearby was Jake's board.
I'd found it! I wasn't doomed after all!

"Hey! That's not a proper skateboard!" the
grumpy judge shouted. I ignored him. As I
ran towards Jake's board, I heard him say
"disqualified", then booing, then Brad shouting
"good!" The crowd started chanting my name.

As I got back to the platform with Jake's board, I realised what had happened. First, I'd been disqualified for not using a proper board. Then the crowd had complained. Then I appeared with Jake's board. So I was back in.

"Get going," the grumpy judge told me. I didn't need telling twice. I slipped Jake's board under my foot and set off. Some ollies, turns, twists – and then it all went wrong.

"Hey, you!" came an angry voice from the crowd.
I looked up and saw Jake. I lost my balance and fell
off. "What have you done with my board?" he yelled.

"Nothing!" I said, holding it up and hoping it
wasn't scratched. "It's here!"

"Oh yeah?" Jake shouted. "Then what's this?"
From behind his back he pulled out an
identical board!

"But where … how … ?" I spluttered.

Brad stepped forward. "I found it outside the shop – *where you left it!*" he said. He had taken the board back to Jake even though he *must* have known that I was inside the shop!

As Jake carried on telling me off, all I could think was: if Jake's got his board back, then whose is *this* one? I soon found out.

"Hey!" another voice shouted from the crowd.

Chapter 5 – The getaway

I saw a group of teenagers with BMX bikes pushing through the crowd. Now, if you're nine, a fourteen-year-old brother can be very scary. A fifteen-year-old stranger can be even scarier, especially if he's got five big mates with him. They all had skateboards strapped to their saddles, except the one doing the shouting. But then how could he have his board? I'd got it!

"I want a word with you!" the scary boy yelled.
I got on my skateplank and tore out of the park.
I was still holding the other boy's skateboard.

The crowd was blocking the bikers but that
wouldn't stop them for long. These boys were
not only BMX-ers, they were streeters as well.
They knew tricks that I could only dream about.

As I gathered speed, I looked back over my shoulder. The bikers had burst through the crowd. Two of them had got off their bikes and were on their boards, heading straight for me. The ones still on bikes split up and headed off in opposite directions.

There was no escape. They were going to sweep round and cut me off.

I reached the
steps down to the
sports centre. The two boys
on boards were almost level with me,
one on either side. They were preparing to
grind along the handrails and block my escape.
My only hope was to jump the steps. I'd never done
this kind of thing, but I had no choice. I reached
the top step, tilted the board and went for it.

The two boys made a grab for me. One fell off onto the grass beside the steps. I did a spin to avoid the other one and landed at the foot of the steps.

Where to now, I wondered? Coming round one side of the sports centre were two girls on bikes. The other bikes were going down the grass beside the steps, cutting me off. Behind me the two boys on boards were closing fast.

If I'd been James Bond, this is when I would
have realised that the skateboard I'd 'borrowed'
was a helicopter. But I wasn't; and it wasn't. It
was an ordinary board that belonged to a scary
boy who was coming towards me, knowing
that I couldn't escape.

I felt like a mouse cornered by a cat. I heard my voice – high and squeaky – burbling an apology. The boy ignored it.

"I think you've got my board," he said. I quickly held it out to him. I was shaking so much that it looked like I was fanning him with it!

"Thanks," he said. He took it, turned round and headed back to his bike. Then he stopped.

He came back really close and gripped my shoulder. "There is one thing," he said quietly in my ear. "Can you teach me that big flippy thing you do? It's way cool!"

I nearly explained that it was called a *Dormer Stormer* and then decided not to. If he wanted to call it a *Big Flippy Thing*, that was fine with me! I managed a weak nod of my head. "Thanks," he said again and walked away.

I couldn't believe it! He wasn't going to hit me!
I had to make sure.

"So, you're not going to … er … punish me
for taking your board?" I asked, trying to sound
casual. He laughed, which made me even more
nervous, especially when his mates joined in.

"Why should I?" he said. "You took it by accident, didn't you?" I nodded frantically. "And I got it back, didn't I?" he added. I nodded so much this time that my head nearly came off.

"Besides," he whispered in my ear, "it's not mine. It's my brother's. But if *you* don't tell him, I won't!"

I just hoped that his brother isn't anything like mine!

"Hey!" yelled a voice from the top of the steps. It was Jake, on his board.

"We need to get back to the skate park," he said. "They're going to announce the winner!" Was he smiling? It looked like it. Brothers are so weird.

So, I wasn't doomed. But I wasn't going to win either. I decided that I might as well go and find out who was. "Race you," Jake said. So I did.

Chapter 7 - The prize

"You've won!" Cassie screamed when we got back to the skate park.

"No, he hasn't. I have!" Brad told her.

It seemed that the judges couldn't decide. Some of them thought I should win. Others thought I should still be disqualified. I moved closer to find out what was going on.

"Yes, but he used an illegal board," Grumpy was saying. (This wasn't fair because *he* was the one that told me to use it in the first place!)

The crowd started chanting, "Ben! Ben! Ben!" In the middle of it, you could just about hear Brad chanting, "Brad! Brad! Brad!"

The judges still could not agree. One of them said, "Which board was the Dormer boy riding when he fell off?"

"A proper one," Grumpy told him.

"And did he fall off when he was riding his homemade board?" the other judge asked.

"No," Grumpy admitted.

"Hmmm," the other one said. "It seems to me that his homemade board is a lot safer than the real thing!"

The chief judge tapped the microphone and held up his hands. The chanting died away, leaving Brad still calling out his own name.

"After much discussion," the judge started. Then he went into lots of technical stuff that I didn't follow. All I heard was, "Bradley Jackson ..."

I fixed a smile and went to congratulate Brad. This was something Dad always insisted on – being a good sport. Brad was looking like the cat with the cream. I held out my hand to shake his.

"… is the runner up," the judge continued to announce. "I therefore declare that the winner is Benjamin Dormer."

The crowd went mad. "Who's that with the weird name?" I thought. Me! It's me! I've won!

"It's not fair!" Brad was shouting at anyone who was listening – which was nobody.

So that's my story. That's how I won the top-of-the-range, state-of-the-art skateboard. It's hanging on my bedroom wall right now. Although it's super-cool, when it comes to stunts – and escaping bigger kids – nothing can beat my Super Skateplank!